Fifteen

D1603523

Fifteen

A Compilation of Poems

Amie Woleslagle

Pixy Publishing

Printed in the United States of America
First Printing, 2020

ISBN:
978-1-7356369-0-0 (paperback)
978-1-7356369-1-7 (ebook)

Poetry
Inspirational/Faith-based Poetry

Pixy Publishing

www.AmieWoleslagle.com

To the Lily

Who grew, flourished, bloomed,
And then wilted away.
May we all remember
The lilies in our garden
Because of her name.

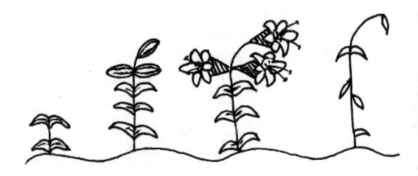

"You keep him in perfect peace
whose mind is stayed on you,
because he trusts in you."

- Isaiah 26:3

Table of Contents

The words goodnight
Scare me to the bone,
They say goodnight
And I say don't leave me alone

They say, "Sleep,
Sleep tight."
But don't you know,
My nightmares come at night.

They say, "Close your eyes
Try to sleep."
But they don't know
The monsters that try to eat me.

Sometimes saying "I'm okay" is the biggest lie you could ever tell. Sometimes, we continue to whisper it to ourselves until we can't ever remember what being okay and fine actually feel like.

IT'S OKAY

It's okay
That's what they all say
Hearts stop beating,
Minds stop singing,
And it's still okay.

Be fine
All of the time
Doesn't matter the pain,
Just keep pretending to be sane
And act fine.

I'm good
Life keeps on, like I knew it would;
Reality pressing down,
A never ending race for the crown,
I'm fine.

Amie Woleslagle

Don't be sad
There's so much to make you glad;
The sun on your skin,
Just let it bring out that grin,
And don't be sad.

Shush.
Don't feel the pain
Pray and let the world hush
There's only one way to feel
Better.

One day
You'll look back on the pain and say
That you're grateful for the chance
To live through this trance
And say

It's okay.

GLITCHING BRAIN

Hum hum hum

An error message overcomes
The thoughts that wrestle in my brain.
Another glitch, another problem
Again, my brain isn't enough for today.

Skip skip skip

Red flashing cues an emergency trip
To save the records stored inside
In a hope that the glitch won't hide
The problems inside my brain.

Delete delete delete

Useless and important alike,
All tossed out of my mind's eye.
Struggling just to finish a single day
Simply because my thoughts won't stay
As the virus takes over my brain.

Repeat repeat repeat

Words I would never have the guts to say
Create a track that my mind focuses on all day
Words that make no sense to me
Bring about panic, exhaustion, and fatigue.
Will my brain ever work for me?

Pause pause pause

Taking a moment to shut my eyes,
Plug my ears and retreat from life.
A nap can bring so much joy inside,
Sorting through thoughts that don't seem so dark
Once my brain is working.

We think being "enough" should be our goal in life, but what if your mental or physical health stops you from doing what you consider "enough?" What are you left with?

Amie Woleslagle

Sometimes, everything can be too much. Sometimes we're fighting the thoughts in our own mind. We don't want to admit that we need help, so we just end up so very confused.

3

CONFUSED

Shush, silence please.
Everything has confused me.

No noise, no questions,
Let me view this situation.

My brain has lost all power,
Let me just sleep another hour.

Insomnia has stolen the real me,
While depression has torn and destroyed me.

Please, don't leave,
I'm scared of the beast within me.

I'm not needy,
So I tell you to leave me

But deep down inside,
I know there's no way to hide

The needs that thrive
In my life.

Amie Woleslagle

Shush, brain stop thinking.

Sleep, come quickly,
Tears, flow smoothly,

Words piece together neatly,
Perhaps it won't happen nightly.

Maybe someday I won't be scared
Of the thoughts that plague me,

Perhaps one day I won't worry
About the people I care for deeply.

Someday may never come
And I'll be left in my shell of a home,

Wondering why this annoys me,
Why can't I be the person I want to be?

Wondering what others see in me,
Wondering why I keep lying.

Is it time I'm buying?
Or is it because I'm denying

The fact that I'm confused,
That I'm not amused,

With the curve balls life has thrown me.

But I'm supposed to be okay
That things aren't going my way.

I'm supposed to relax,
I'm supposed to let go,

Instead I increase my hold
And ruin the show.

So now I sit silently,
Wondering how I can do it rightly,

And ending up so very confused.

Amie Woleslagle

We are told that tears are weak. We're not supposed to cry, we're supposed to be strong, to have it all together. But sometimes, tears are the truest strength. And sometimes, hiding the tears is the quickest way to hurt yourself and others.

TEARS

Hot face,
Give me space,
My heart needs more time.

In the dark,
I lack the spark,
To laugh at the life before me.

Salt grazes,
Water phases,
Life finally allows this release.

Hard walls,
Reality calls,
I push the emotions away.

Embrace the tears
Push, tug, lug the fears
Because at the end of the dark day

The tears
Wash the pain away,
And help you see the reason to stay.

Amie Woleslagle

Grief and mental pain can be like asthma, while people we love can relieve the pain like an inhaler. But at the end of the day, if they leave, it all feels just like a dream as the pain returns.

5

ASTHMATIC

Wheeze
Life is shorter than it seems.
Breathe
Worry pressing until all I need is
Air
Oxygen does not exist, every breath
Pants
Wishing for some advance, wishing I wasn't an
Asthmatic

Inhale
Black spots taunt me in front of my face.
Exhale
The world is tilting, spinning all around,
Help
Unable to do it myself,
Gasp
This breath might be my last.
Asthmatic

Amie Woleslagle

Whisper
You are soothing like my inhaler.
Puff
Ease my struggles, stop my sufferings,
Sigh
Nothing tastes as good as your gentle ease,
Stir
You aren't leaving me?
Asthmatic

Gulp
Fill my lungs with a whiff of you,
Sigh
I knew it was too good to be true.
Sniff
Left without a reason why
Inspire
Was this just another delirious dream
Of an Asthmatic

We all fear something.
Maybe our something is big,
maybe our something is
small. In the end,
regardless of size or
importance, we either have
control of our fears, or
our fears have control over
us.

METAL CHAINS

Fear's metal chains
Increase your mental pains,
Adding restrictions
To already tight obligations.

One moment you think
Fear has left you to sink
Down below the surface
To the inferno-infested place.

Heartbeat quickens
As everything thickens,
Plot, pace, the world's a mess
Never letting you rest.

Fear is your master,
Though it should be your slave
Take a deep breath
And confront it today.

Amie Woleslagle

Mental illness creates a void. A hole between the world around you and the world inside of you. Only you can see that hole, and so those around you often don't understand the battle and pain within.

VOID

The darkness in my head is numb
Breaking my knees, forcing me to succumb
To the voice inside my head,
Whispering there is no end.

Lights shimmer around my soul
But I'm blinded by this ghoul
Each movement robotic,
Each heartbeat chaotic.

Breathe, let oxygen purge me
Sigh, exhale the gloom inside me
Feel, focus on reality
Taste, know that there is a world beside me.

Life with this darkness seems too long,
It grows into a dense throng
My mind can't shake it,
My heart can't take it.

There has to be something to quiet inside,
Will the gospel cease the never ending tide?
Will I release the dark thoughts that have toyed
With my soul in the never-ending void?

Society creates the best freak show, where we are forced to mold our crafts to fit in with the regulations of society, all the while begging to be free from the expectations it places on us and the labels it uses.

FREAK SHOW

Welcome to my freak show
Where creatures untold
Deliver horrors yet unknown.

Devils darker than tales of time
Take time to deliver a gold mine
Of talents to the holy shrine.

Welcome to my freak show,
Everyone ought to know
That these talents are unwillingly bestowed.

Time spent to perfect the craft
Some threaten to abandon the raft
But to my cause their souls are lashed.

Songs sung in a minor key,
Bodies changing to fit and agree
All because they want to be free.

Free from my freak show.

Five times you say go away
For you don't have time today
You three have plans
Too busy for me
Maybe if I just had one day
I'd plan to stay.

You said that I didn't have to stay
Where would I go, alone all day?

Amie Woleslagle

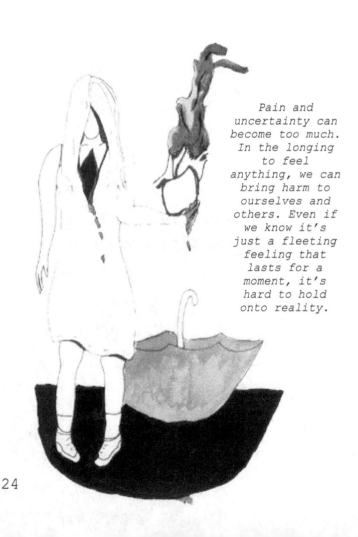

Pain and uncertainty can become too much. In the longing to feel anything, we can bring harm to ourselves and others. Even if we know it's just a fleeting feeling that lasts for a moment, it's hard to hold onto reality.

PAIN AWAY

Please just fix it.
Heal the hurt in my heart
Or just burn it,
So I won't fall apart.

Each day brings the same mistakes.
Repeating the pain
 And wondering what it takes
To stop this awful train.

Will I crash?
Will I burn?
Or can I smash
And can I learn?

Is it over?
Or has it just begun?
Will this strengthen?
Or will I be done?

Can I live?
Or will I die?
Is each moment mine?
Or in silence will I lie?

Gloriously living each moment,
Each day
Or quietly wishing
To forever silent lay.

Victory is mine
But I didn't pay
The price of the gift
Of success that day.

But the question is rough
Can I trust
The Word and the Will
Of my Heavenly King?

The pain is more real
More tangible I feel,
Than the promises of
Hope and peace.

The darkness veils,
The pain quails,
And over all I can say
It isn't any good this way.

So please let me hang on
To one more day
Please just stop
And take the pain away.

QUIET

You're so quiet,
You're so thin,
Your eyes are vacant
Lacking the soul within.

Speak some more,
Throw back your head and grin
Dance to the music
And find the soul within.

Why don't you listen?
Why don't you speak?
Holding it in,
As the emotions leak.

Why do you shake
Your head and sigh?
Why do you refuse
To tell me why?

Amie Woleslagle

I won't ignore you,
Your small voice will be heard.
Don't worry, child,
Whisper the word.

No one cares
About your mental pain?
No one worries
Or listens when you call their name?

Child, let me in.
Darling, give me a chance
To hear the story,
Don't judge me at a glance.

You're deeper than your problems,
Stronger than your fears,
Worth more than your gifts
And allowed to shed tears.

I will be silent,
I will be trying,
To hear your story
So you don't have to be dying.

We just want someone to notice our pain,
letting anyone who promises to take it away.
When a soft spoken human comes and says they
understand, giving us a hand, we feel like
giving in, regardless of who they are or
what extra pain they may give.

Amie Woleslagle

We often hold onto other people's anger when we have no business carrying it at all. In the end, we have to remember that it's not our responsibility to hold onto another person's anger.

THE ANGER

The anger you give
Burns my soul,
To see the pain you create
And the horrors you've told.

You say the way the world rotates
Will forever remain the same,
Telling me to change or relocate.

But my dear friend,
My voice cannot be silenced,
There will be no violence
But I shall still be heard.

Truth carries farther than the lies
Just wait for the final sunrise
And the anger you give will die.

Amie Woleslagle

Pain added to anger makes a crippling load, and when it's not even your own, it wounds your soul.

YOUR PAIN

Why are you adding pain
To my humble name?
Why are you pressing,
Seeing what you can gain?

I've been told to let you go,
Ignoring the ache that grows.
You weren't worth knowing
So why should I hurt so?

Losing friends isn't the end
Loneliness shouldn't send
Your mind down a dark path,
Searching and unable to find.

But my breath and will are gone,
It's been so extremely long
Since someone asked me to spill
All the tears to which I hold on.

Amie Woleslagle

Why did you do this to me?
Why am I doing this to myself?
I can't let you go, can I?
Why am I holding onto your pain?

Sometimes we have people who we call "friends," but in the end, they never meant to be anyone that we could trust. They leave us with a hole, with pain and anger, but just because they left it doesn't mean we have to keep the extra load.

13

GHOSTS

As a kid they told me ghosts weren't real
But your presence is enough to kill
Dead already, a living ghoul
What did you do to my poor soul?

Called me friend, yet stole my heart
Drew me in, then threw the dart
Told me you'd stay
Only to crush my heart.
Time to cut the strings while you depart.

Bled my veins, the numbness overrided
Every minute, my heart is more divided.
Give me life, awake my bones
I'm not ready to go, don't you know?

Called me friend, yet stole my heart
Drew me in, then threw the dart
Told me you'd stay
Only to break my heart.
Shush, it's time for you to depart.

Amie Woleslagle

Every moment you tore me in two
Half of me truly loved you
Anxiety, agony, let me go free
I told you, just please, let me be.

Called me friend, yet stole my heart
Drew me in, then threw the dart
Told me you'd stay
Only to depart.
Hello, leave my heart.

Called me friend, yet left me hanging
Drew me in, yet left a hole gaping
Told me you'd stay
Just to confirm you're a liar.
Goodbye, as a friend, you're fired.

*Our body can be so heavy, so weak, so sick. Our
mind can sometimes just decide to quit. Even
though we long to cross through heaven's doors,
God requires us to finish our race on earth.*

14

MORTAL FRAME

Missing those who've gone before
Wishing death would come knock on the door

Tears are gone, dried forever,
Leaving my heart in complete terror.

Why must the earth hold on?
Will this agony go on for long?

Why can't I go and wait for others to come?
Why must I stay here for another day?

Fire eats my mind until it is just ash,
Numbness fills my soul until I can't look past

The lack of pain inside my frame.
Bones burn with an eternal flame,

I'm going down
Going down.

Goodbye
My mortal frame.

15

MARIONETTE

Empty, hollow, reverb follows
Ticking creates my melody,
For my friend
I am simply
A marionette on vibrating strings.

One leg lifts, but my nerves don't feel
Allowing my arms to sag in defeat,
For my friend
I am empty.
A piece of wood on vibrating strings.

Head rests on the chilly wall,
My sight focusing on how I can fall,
For my friend
I am afraid.
A breakable toy on vibrating strings.

Maybe life was once inside,
But now I crumple, I have died,
For my friend
I am numb.
A block of ice on vibrating strings.

My fingers tingle, my arm moves,
Maybe I am still alive, perhaps I'm not doomed,
For my friend
I am breathing.
A dying human on vibrating strings.

A soft hand touches my waxen face,
Arms tighten in a life-giving embrace,
For my friend
I am loved.
A work of art on vibrating strings.

At times, we can't feel ourselves or our emotions. Everything is numb, and we feel as if our reactions are dictated by someone else outside of us. As if we are just wooden figures on a string.

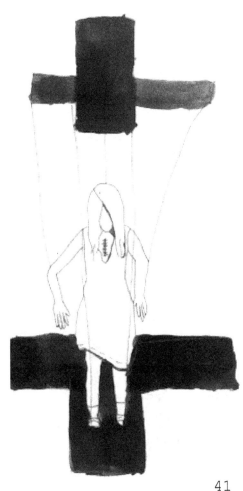

Amie Woleslagle

In all of our mental health journeys, we've had that day where we wake up and realize that we don't want to be ourselves anymore. We don't want to spend the rest of our lives living the way we are living. And so? We pen our resolutions, and decide that we won't be ourselves anymore.

16

ANYMORE

Tear drops,
Long droughts,
Forgetting this life's thoughts
One thing keeps coming
One thought keeps running
I don't want to be you
I don't want to see you
I don't want to free you
Anymore.

Long nights,
Wakeful eyes,
I keep reliving
Every mistake in my being
And I keep screaming
I don't want to be you
I don't want to hear you
I don't want to be near you
Anymore.

Muttered whispers,
Overheard titters,
I know I'm strange
Just let me outta range
I don't need to hear your thoughts
I don't want to be you
I don't want to know you
I don't want to show you
Anymore.

Deep breaths,
Loud heaves,
I don't need the advice
Can't you see I'm getting along just fine
Doing it my way as I say
I don't want to be you
I don't want to hurt you
I don't want to burn you
Anymore.

Fresh ink,
I think,
You ought to hear my new resolves
You have to see that you'll really be
Better off without me
I don't want to be you
I don't want to leave you
I don't want to scar you
Anymore.

Tight fists,
I insist,
Yeah I know this hurts
But it also cures
We don't have to be in pain forever
I don't have to keep saying
I don't have to keep praying
I won't be you
Anymore.

One tear more
Drops on the floor,
Just one more sigh
As the time goes by.

Sorrow never leaves,
It stays and cleaves
To the roots of your heart
And tears you apart.

One thought by one thought,
The sorrows life brought
Keep you from doing your part
In this world.

Amie Woleslagle

We have to fight.
We don't win this fight by giving into the
voice in our head, the numbness in our mind.
We don't beat it by giving up or giving in,
we beat it by living. By gloriously living
until God calls us home to be with Him.

17

FIGHT

Endless thoughts whirl round and round,
Feet set firmly on the ground.

Quiet voices echoing,
Trying to voice what they're wondering.

Topics that should never be discussed,
Handled in one long rush.

Time will continue its race,
But my time will end and I'll see God's face.

What words will drip from my lips
When my life from this to the next slips?

Will I hear the longed for refrain?
Or will I have to take the dreaded train?

Death seems like a sweet relief,
But I've seen that it is but a thief.

Stop your endless whining,
Someday you'll see there's no reason to be crying.

Watch, and you just might
See the beauty in this fight.

18

STAY

Your heartbeat slows
You're begging to let go,
But take a moment to hear
Your end isn't near
So please stay.

Your mind's given up
Don't let your emotions mix up
Fantasy and life's reality,
People need your personality
So please stay.

Critics back up your mind's words
But I'm here to show that though it hurts,
You don't have to go
Repeat until you know
You'll stay.

Every moment, every day
Keep running the race
Someday you'll awake
And realize that for my sake
You stayed.

People complain about
their names. They can't
seem to understand that at
birth, they were given a
gift, a gift that would be
theirs throughout the
years. A gift that no one
can take away. You will
always have your name, and
there's nothing else you
can say that about.

YOUR NAME

What is in a name?
Strings of syllables
Tied into a sound of fame,
Attached to something physical.

Meaning hidden behind the word
Identity wrapped around a noise
Sharing with the whole world
Your parent's simple choice.

Trying to match the word that defines
As you experiment with emotions.
Does the name confine
Or push you into a motion?

Years pass by on the wings of time
That word still is yours
As all else has lost it's rhyme,
That word is still yours.

Time can't steal it from you,
Pain can't do the same.
And even death can't rid you
Of what is in your name.

We are told by so many
different people what
is good and what is bad
for our mental and
physical health. But in
the end, we have to
decide on our own what
works.

20

EXPRESSO

Dark the brew that calms the storm,
Gentle the taste that caresses my tongue.

Images dance before my eyes,
Entrancing my taste buds and overruling my lies.

Smooth and clear as it awakens my senses,
Bringing reality into my presence.

Dark the liquid that lights up my life
Light the cream that enhances it twice.

Billows of caffeine covers my need,
Softly the trickle continues to ease.

People whisper and tell me to stop,
Caffeine can't be healthy, you can't drink a lot.

But if it heals the hurt in my soul,
If it continues to make me whole,

Is it truly terrible to drink a cup?
Can't you please just understand it picks up

My drooping spirits and hurting head,
And the thoughts that continue spread.

Whisper, please, and let me have another drink
It keeps me above water, it helps me not to sink.

*We don't think.
Every moment we react to
what is going on around
us, we take, we survive,
and in the end, have we
really tried? Are we
really stronger for what
we have done? Or are we
the losers who have done
nothing at all?*

21

JUST TRY

What's your fate?
Sitting there to take, take, take,
Never giving thought
To those who have fought,
And all of the pain
That flows through others' veins
While you write, write, write,
Ignoring others fight,
Sucked in your own sob story
While songs of your own vainglory
Ring through your ears
You can't see what's near.

What's your call?
Standing there tall, tall, tall
Complaining about the smallest thing
While others are in great need
All of that time
Wasted like a crime
As you wait, wait, wait
Taking a break
As others bleed and die
And you keep wondering why
The world is dark.
You're blinded to all in life that hurts.

Stop denying it all.
Let yourself cry, cry, cry
And stop asking the question why.
Instead keep your eyes on the goal
And minister to the soul,
Love is the salve
And you should never give doses in halves.
Just try, try, try
Doesn't have to always be right
Just don't give up the fight
Keep on with all your might
Just try.

ISOLATION

Souls crave for peace and silence above ground
A soft blanket to cover you all around
But when all's quiet,
There's no option about it,
Isolation grows old.

Loneliness is the curse of mankind
Driving men to do things unjust to find
A helping hand
To rescue from sinking sand,
Isolation is insane.

Thoughts are amplified when our eyes
Fail to land on a human's gentle face,
We begin to doubt
Our reality throughout,
Isolation is a desperate place.

Stark white, blinding dark, it all becomes the same
When we struggle to keep our wits and stay sane,
We wonder if we exist
Or if we're just a wish
When Isolation has control.

Reason is defied when the only humans in our eyes
Are brought to us through a colorful screen.
We long for a touch,
For just one more lunch
Before Isolation disturbed the scene.

Friends live miles away,
Making us wonder why we stay
Locked up inside
Perhaps we shouldn't hide
Maybe we should lock Isolation away.

A voice is better than the ring of silence,
A bouquet in love better than lonely crying,
Even if they're far away
Our hearts are closer than I can say
We snub Isolation with defiance.

I don't need people.
I like to think I'm all alone in the world
and that I prefer it that way. But isolation
is a mind-numbing life-sucker. Even if we
can't have friends who live next door, we
can still have people who care miles away.

From watching Disney movies, to reading magazines, to scrolling social media, we all know what the perfect body is supposed to look like. And yet, none of us have it. Some of us do terrible things to achieve it, but even with all that, we aren't as beautiful as we are told to be, encased in tutus and tights and silhouetted by dazzling stage lights. However, we are each imperfectly beautiful in our own ways.

TUTUS AND TIGHTS

Bodies encased in tutus and tights,
Perfection glistens with stage lights.
Movements tick by with gilded wings,
Society tells us what we should be.

Bodies sculpted instead of just made,
Bodies tortured to fit the standard of clay.
Society is not the only beast,
Women tell lies to each other and feast.

Corpses of forsaken bodies lay
Out in a warning parade,
These once acknowledged icons
Now outdated, neglected, and spit on.

If we but achieve characteristics not our own,
Lengthen our legs and tighten our bum,
Fill out our lips and cinch our waist,
Perhaps perfection will be attained today.

If your eyes could behind the curtain peek
Perhaps we would all be able to see
The tears that drip off the sculpted nose
And the calluses that line their perfect toes.

Thin lips and chunky hips should never bring shame,
Beauty changes from age to age,
But one thing will always remain
Faith, hope, and charity add beauty that will stay.

BREATHE

Deep breath
Calm mind
Stay grounded
Leave the world within.

Focus outward
Do not think
Of the future
Or of unknown things.

Music without
Sounds within,
Colors flash,
When will it all begin?

Shush, silence your thinking
Hush, quiet your heart's beating.
Run away from your mind.
We're all here, we're outside.

Speak, don't hold it in,
Sing, let the music begin.
Leave, the thoughts will go
You'll be better, you know.

Don't give up
You're not over, just trust
God has plans
Patience is what he demands.

Trust, let it go
Praise, let the music flow
Thank, His goodness is clear
He continues to draw you near

So breathe
Let the music steal your feet
You aren't leaving, not today
So breathe.

I forgot how to breathe.
It's so easy to hold your
breath, to move and push until
air no longer exists. Until we
are just broken shells without
oxygen. But once we let out our
hot air, we begin to be able to
appreciate everything elsewhere.

67

We forget the beauty in life.
We forget that once upon a time, we believed
in fairytales before we lost ourselves. Life
doesn't require us to forget the stars when
we sleep through the night. Instead, it
gives us sunshine.

25

FATE

Feet move to a gentle beat,
Laughter grows at a steady increase;
Keep your eyes on the goal
And the music will help your soul.

The floor isn't quite so cold,
The peace floods your heart.
Small moments slip by
as you're locked in your mind.

Sunlight dances across your face,
Invading your personal space
And letting your mind give a chance
To the music that lets you dance.

Breath release, open your eyes to see
Glitter and pixie dust raining on you,
Fly to the moon, reach for the stars
Allow people to love you as you are.

Find out who you are and sing,
Let your own melody ring,
And run to the sound you create
As you accept your own fate.

26

HOPE AND FEAR NOT

Hanging quotes upon my wall
Overlapping colors, creating songs
Previous memories swirl along
End in creating a unique anatonal.

Anyone may see my quotes on the wall,
Not understanding what they mean at all
Doesn't matter to me, as long as they understand my peace.

Five quotes explain presence of my mind
Each one encourages, push and challenging mine,
A simple word can carry so much, letters
Revealing the heart of the people I touch.

There hangs pictures of those I love
Holding memories and dreams in a gentle glove,
Other thoughts push and pull for my time,
Unique dreams and ambitions I've fought to call mine.

Now you tilt your head to view the masterpiece
Over my bed it sits complete,
To remind me to never give into defeat.

Beyond my wall, the treasures hang in my heart
Every time I give up it reminds me to restart
Life may be full of defeat and grief,
Only the darkness in this journey you may see.
Vibrato might shake your mind every day,
Even destroy the castles you've built in your brain,
Darling, just remember, hope and fear thou not,
beloved.

Hope is a foreign thing.
Fear is in everything.
The idea of being beloved is foreign.
And yet, we are told to hope and fear not,
because we are beloved and can trust in
Christ's assured hope.

A year slips by
It feels so new
Before it's broken in
It's another year's cue.

Lessons learned
Yet not understood
Memories made
And others erased.

Hearts broken
Eyes red-rimmed
But flowers bloom
In spite of gloom.

Charred ashes gather,
Emptiness blossoms into flower.

Amie Woleslagle

Face your fears.
Whether that's heights, performing
in front of people, or even just
calling someone you don't often
talk to. Shake your fears, and
you'll realize that they don't have
as strong as hold over you as you
first thought.

27

RAPPEL

The sight before my eyes wavers
The height seems to extend,
My stomach flips and quavers
Hoping my mind won't do it in the end.

Up one step, don't look down
Two steps, don't think about how far from the ground
Comfort zone is miles behind
This is new territory I'm forced to climb.

Half way up, and I feel it shake,
My stomach drops to my feet in a rush
Why did I think this would be a piece of cake?
The top is in sight, my knees feel weak.

Knots are tied around my waist as I refuse to look
down,
Jokes cracked and I slowly walk off
My boots vertical with the ground
And I walk down.

Amie Woleslagle

Feet slip, gravity wins
I'm hanging upside down.
Words surround me, muscles strain
While I just take a moment to look around.

Fear vanishes without a trace
If I can defy gravity without pain
Then why should I worry about my fate?
I'll just wait.

Strong arms pull the rope, I'm upright
And I let go,
I'm living, I'm all right,
Flying down the wall and I know.

Fears and hate and lust abound
Assumptions and discredit are all around,
At times you might hang upside down,
But in the end, you'll be pulled.

And you'll have a choice to stay where you are,
Or you have a choice to let go and go far
Fear might yell and shout and babble
But you can still let go and rappel.

28

SINKING SAND

Peers could care less about spiritual things,
Media that portrays us as evil beings,
A fear that faith will cripple your dreams.

Darkness shrouding everything you see
Moments tick by, creating an endless sea
Your heart beat is numbered by the King.

The faith of your forefathers isn't enough
Not when the heat and hate turn up
The choice is in your hands and yours alone.

Faith isn't an obligated thing
Instead of you, the rocks could sing
But will you shout from the rooftops?

Your faith must be your everything
Silence should no longer be an option as you think
Of when you view your destiny.

Will you be a rock against the flood waters?
Will you take a stand for all that really matters?
Or is life to you a simple dream?

Amie Woleslagle

Sand is gentle, sand is soft
Sand is easy to mold but ought
You really risk your everything

On sinking sand where salvation isn't a thing?

We hate to be different than our peers, and yet we've been taught that our faith is the answer to everything. A half hearted faith will heal no hurt, pleasing both peers and God is impossible and exhausting. So who will you serve?

Amie Woleslagle

You are special. There are a million different ways to describe the angles of your personality. Never forget that in the end, you are beautiful. Every single angle has something precious to it.

THE BOOK

Dark night sky,
Laughter in her bright eyes,
Moody silences
Brooding looks,
It's all a part of the same book.

Mid-morning sunshine,
Bluegrass and white wine,
Songs spring,
Lights gleams,
It's all a part of the same book.

Moonlight,
Sorrow dark as night
Tears hidden
Pain observed
It's all a part of the same book.

Amie Woleslagle

Curls, twirls, interesting words,
Blue and pink adding to the world
Minor keys
Everyone sees
It's all a part of the same book.

Reality covers their eyes,
Yet fairies dance in their minds,
Non-stop talking
And giggling
It's all a part of the same book.

Paint covered canvas
Ink on your hands
It's amazing what artist adventures
This one can have,
In the same book.

30

LULLABY

Gentle, the raindrops wash away my tears,
The warmth quiets my fears.

Heat loosens my muscles, easing my pain
Washing away the assumptions on my name.

Grief, pain, fears, anxiety, depression,
Water washes away their deepening impression.

Humid air fills my lungs,
Letting go of the trouble that to everyone belongs.

My heart beat slows, letting in peace
The tangled web of thoughts cease.

Lavender scent soothes and fills my nose
Bringing gentle thoughts that help me repose.

Rough and warm, the towel dries,
Wiping away thousands of lies.

My mind is a liar and it continues to deceive,
But tonight the thoughts are quiet and leave.

Amie Woleslagle

Fluffy socks kiss my raw feet,
My bed sinks as I take a seat.

Moments like these are beautiful and sweet
However sad and quickly they flee.

Learning to accept and hold these memories
Without dwelling on my mind's treachery.

Tonight sleep seems in my grasp
Tonight I will hold it to my heart in a tight clasp.

Flicker, gentle, let the world whisper
Relax my limbs and let out a shiver.

Breathing, being, closing my eyes
Now it is time to whisper goodnight.

*Sleep, rest, and peace can seem impossible,
but there are the short lived moments that
we can just let out everything. In those
moments, we feel peace. Cling to those
moments, treasure them, and remember them,
and let a smile bloom from them.*

Amie Woleslagle

Who are you?
There is so much beautifulness and
uniqueness bottled up inside each of us,
like pixie dust. Find your pixie dust and
let it seep out of your personality.

31

PIXIE DUST

Glitter, flitter, laughter fills my dreams,
Rainbow colors cover the seams.

Fluorescent lights cover up the dark,
Shading makes the black ever less stark.

Quiet, quiet all the loud lies,
Smile, smile, as we explore all of life's ties.

Giggles bubble from the fountain inside,
Adding to the music of the outgoing tide.

White teeth curve into a crescent moon,
Outlined by lips that curve up at the lightest tune.

Joy bounds for the warmth of the eyes,
And these are only some of the mysteries

Of the pixie dust flung into the girl's personality.

Amie Woleslagle

*We feel numb.
But someday, when the ice
melts and the sorrow lifts,
we will see the sunshine.
We will hear the birds
again, we will laugh and
let the breeze ruffle our
hair. It isn't always
winter, this season too
will pass.*

32

SUNSHINE

Sunshine, bird song,
All sadness flew along.
Bright laughter, white teeth,
Everything is as sweet as it seems.

Cellos play on this glorious day,
Sit down here, let us stay.
A soft flute, the tiny gong,
The day is sweet and long.

Tears dry, wounds heal,
Every moment is full of appeal.
Grass so soft, the leaves so green,
A log upon which we can lean.

Soft the wind, loud the peace,
My heart beat slowly begins to increase.
Let the breath slowly release,
For this, my friend, is spring.

Amie Woleslagle

Sometimes it takes months,
sometimes it takes days.
Sometimes it'll never totally
go away, but hope will bloom in
the ashes of your pain. You
will be stronger, and you will
someday look back and know that
there was a reason you suffered
through those dark days.

33

FIFTEEN

Seasons come and go
Bringing lessons to show
The notes of this life's song.

One year taught you that life's a lonely road
And can be taken easy and slow,
There's no race to finish, so slow your frantic pace.

Two years were taken up in teaching you to cry
The hours it took, the things you tried
To dry up the tears when all you needed was a hearty
cry.

Three times you had to hear people whisper in your
ear
That they were near, to breathe and take in
everything here
As four tears slide down your nose.

Five days is barely time to learn
About the peace which every soul learns,
But six marked the bitter end of that brief lesson.

Amie Woleslagle

Seven years of pain, my heart bleeding out
Eight months of agony, fighting against doubt
My soul is exhausted, giving up all throughout.

Ten, a number full of hope,
But that was before darkness pulled the rope
Leaving me to wander empty and alone.

Eleven was the start of my downward spiral
Twelve breaths were left, how long is awhile?
The thirteenth breath, all's black and stone within.

Fourteen breaks the spell, and I have grown
The sun shines within and reveals all I've known
Brain and heart might be apart, but both have won
the battle.

The tears watered the flower that ended in bloom,
Reaching towards the sun when the hour struck noon
A flower whose petals numbered fifteen.

"For he wounds, but he binds up;
He shatters, but his hand heals."
- Job 5:18

Note from the Author

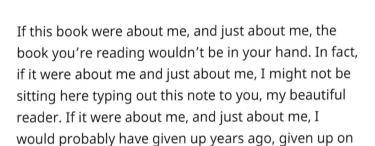

If this book were about me, and just about me, the book you're reading wouldn't be in your hand. In fact, if it were about me and just about me, I might not be sitting here typing out this note to you, my beautiful reader. If it were about me, and just about me, I would probably have given up years ago, given up on everything.

But praise the Lord, it's not about me, and it's not just me.

God calls us to do hard things for Him. His first call was to give myself to Him, and years later, it was a call to keep living when everything else inside me asked to die. And this year? One of the calls was to publish a poetry book of the lessons that He has taught me. A book to help other teens dealing with mental health issues.

This book isn't just about mental health issues. It's not just about broken, bleeding hearts and hope. It's about one simple word. *Love*.

Love is what has kept me alive. At first, it was love for my parents, knowing that I couldn't hurt them. Then it became love for Christ, love for myself, and over time, it has overflowed and become love for you. For other teens like me. For the hurting.

But if it were about me and just me, I wouldn't have that love. The only reason I have love for you, love for my parents, love for myself is because Jesus Christ first loved me. Sounds kinda strange, right? But it's true. And once you realize that and let that love wash over you, fill you, and overflow through you, you'll understand. You'll understand why I wrote this book, why I'm still alive, and ultimately why you should live, too. Because it's all about His love.

All the hearts,

~~Amie~~

Acknowledgements

This is my favorite part of the book, the part where I can tell everyone how awesome they are. It's hard to go through all the memories and pull out names. It's hard to take the pressing, thundering emotion of gratitude and put it into words for people to read and understand. Because without these people, you wouldn't be holding this book, so put it down and give a round of applause to them.

First, I must thank Angela Lee. We both had no idea that when I asked for a project to work on, it would turn into this. Thank you for being there for me, and for persisting, even when I continued to push you away.

Secondly, I must thank Savannah Morello. Girl, without you, this book would still be a doc on my computer. You've been able to deal with my anxiety, listening to me, but always pushing just enough to keep me going. I always said I knew we would work well together, and this has just proved it. You're amazing.

I must thank my family for all they have put into this project and my writing journey. For their support, love, and the fun rhyming games we played together. Thank you for putting up with my highs and lows, for being stable even when the world seems to crumble. God knew you were just the family I needed.

A huge shout-out to those wonderful people on my email list, the beautiful people who wouldn't let me settle for just a freebie, but instead pushed me to aim for what I considered impossible. You continue to make me smile with your support, encouragement, and excitement about the things I do. Your excitement is contagious and I wouldn't exchange it for anything.

I also want to thank my blogging community. You guys have seen me grow up, and many of you have grown up with me. I would love to meet each one of you, give you guys a hug, and let you know all that your comments and support has meant over the years. When I felt like I had lost myself, you stood there and told me it was okay to wait for myself to come back.

Lastly, but not at all leastly, I need to thank YOU. You, the reader. Thank you for picking up this book, for letting this dream become a reality. I pray that this has greatly encouraged you.

All the hearts,

~~Amie~~

You Want More?

I'm always bummed at the end of books, especially if I loved them. I want more, and I want to find a way to learn more about the author and their writing processes. If you're anything like me, you're in luck!

If you want to find out more about Fifteen, what I've been up to, my next writing news, which podcasts I've been honored to be a guest on, and other fun things, I have something for you.

AmieWoleslagle.com
(a website of all those goodies)

And if you want to help me out, go leave a review for *Fifteen* on its Amazon or GoodReads page. I'm an indie author, so I appreciate every bit of love and interaction with my readers. It always brightens my day to see your sweet reviews or comments.

You're wondering how you can receive early news about my different projects? I'm glad you are! Join my email list and become one of my Newsies to receive personal emails from yours truly. You can sign up on my website, AmieWoleslagle.com.

You can also connect with me on these platforms.
Instagram: @writingamieanne
YouTube: @amieanne
Thank you so much! Hope on, and continue to shine.
All the hearts,
~~Amie~~

About the Author

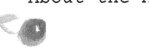

Amie is a suburban cowgirl with a penchant for words. Though her writing started as a coping mechanism, it quickly became a burning passion to

help others defeat the same challenges she faces. Battling with physical and mental health issues, she is passionate about showing through her stories and poetry that in the darkest night, the stars shine the brightest.

Amie loves to run barefoot through southern fields, grow corn, blog, act, film YouTube videos, play music filled with dynamics, and sing at the top of her lungs when no one's listening. All the while, she babies her dog and rabbit, and gasps whenever a new idea floats into her head.

If you would like to connect with Amie, you can find her pouring out her heart on her blog, fangirling about books on her Instagram, or diving into story and goofing off on her YouTube.